NIGEL KENDALL'S
DRAGONFLY
DISCOVERIES

This book of images is a cross section of the many species of dragonflies and damselflies I have encountered over the past 20 years.

These beautiful and dynamic insects are a passion in my life and I have spent many hours seeking out different species from many countries. Hopefully you will enjoy these portraits as much as I have enjoyed compiling them.

© Nigel Kendall 2020

"The dragonfly brings dreams to reality and is the messenger of wisdom and enlightenment from other realms"

Emerald Damselfly

I found my first Emerald Damselflies at a pool among the spoil heaps at Priddy Mineries - ancient Roman lead workings in Somerset.
Preferred habitats of this species are pools, ponds and moorlands. It is a species of still or very slow flowing water. The emerald damselfly has a large Palaeartic distribution, and is found in a band across central Europe and Asia from Spain to the Pacific. It is not found in the far north in Europe and Asia or in the extreme south, being absent from southern Spain, southern Italy and Greece. It is probably found in some areas of north Africa, and where it occurs around the Mediterranean it is found at altitude. In Great Britain it is the only Lestes species that is common.

Golden-ringed Dragonfly

The Golden-ringed Dragonfly is a large, striking dragonfly and the longest British species. It is the only member of its genus to be found in the United Kingdom, breeding in acidic rivers and streams of all sizes. May also be found away from its breeding habitat, over heathland.

My first Golden-ringed Dragonfly was at Landacre Bridge in the middle of Exmoor.

The species is easily identified by their distinctive black and yellow stripes, which no other dragonfly in the United Kingdom has. They are often seen flying leisurely over mountain streams or river, and also occasionally show up at a pond. Golden-ringed Dragonflies can also be seen flying over heathland.

This striking insect is an incredibly aerobatic and they sometimes fly very high in the sky.

White-legged Damselfly

The White-legged Damselfly or Blue Featherleg is a damselfly of slow-flowing, muddy waters. It occurs from the Atlantic to Siberia and is often abundant throughout its range.

My first encounter with the species was by the River Isle in west Somerset. It is the only small damselfly with white and feather-like legs.

Floodplains, rivers, and open stretches of streams, are typical habitats for White-legged Damselflies. Also lakes and a wide range of man-made habitats, like canals, gravel pits and fish ponds.

Ruby Meadowhawk

The Ruby Meadowhawk is a species in the family Libellulidae. It is found in the northern United States and Southern Ontario, Canada. Adult males are identifiable by a distinctive orange to brown face and red bodies. Female faces have the same colours as males. Bodies are brown to dark-red.

The species inhabits temporary ponds, sometimes permanent, and marshes; occasionally lakes, swamps, bogs and stream backwaters. It forages around weed stems in the open and basks on the ground.

I found Ruby Meadowhawks in lakeside vegetation at Snyder Flats, and Columbia Lake in the grounds of Waterloo University, Ontario.

Emperor Dragonfly

My first Emperor was quite a thrill. With its bright blue abdomen and green thorax it made quite an impression on me, and still does today.

This dragonfly has a wide distribution. It is found throughout Africa and through most of Europe, the Arabian Peninsula, and south-western and central Asia. Since 2000, its range has expanded in Europe, both northwards and to higher altitudes.

They breed in a variety of aquatic habitats from large ponds to dikes, but they require a plentiful supply of vegetation in the water. The adult male is highly territorial and difficult to approach. In the summer months Emperor Dragonflies are frequent visitors to gardens, being especially prevalent in the southern counties of Great Britain.

Ruddy Darter

The Ruddy Darter is to be found in temperate regions throughout Europe as far east as Siberia and as far south as the northern Sahara.

This species tends to prefer quiet bodies of water that feature semi-aquatic vegetation such as rushes and reeds. It tends to avoid running or acidic waters but lush vegetation seems to be a key requirement.

I first found a Ruddy Darter beside a pool among the spoil heaps of an ancient Roman lead mine in Somerset.

Brown Hawker

The Brown Hawker is probably the most easily identifiable Hawker in flight. A mere glimpse is often sufficient for a positive identification. It is generally a heavy, brown-bodied and amber-winged dragonfly, often seen gliding down forest glades or over woodland lakes.

The species is most common at higher elevations in northern Europe and it prefers to breed in a wide range of calm waters, usually with rich banks or submerged vegetation such as abandoned canals, oxbows and fenland.

I found my first Brown Hawkers in the valley woodlands of the Somerset Levels.

Eastern Forktail

This species is present in the Eastern United States, from the Atlantic coast to the Midwest, north of Florida to Southern Canada and west to Montana and New Mexico.

These damselflies inhabit various wetlands, especially small ponds, slow moving streams and marshes. They have a slender body with four wings folding over the back. The thorax of the males is black above, with pale blue sides and blue shoulder stripes. Females are usually greyish-blue, with greyish markings on the abdomen but may be less commonly yellow-green like the male.

This species is very similar to the Western Forktail, but the two species can be separated on the basis if their range. I found them at Laurel Creek Conservation near Waterloo, Ontario.

Small Red Damselfly

The Small Red Damselfly is a small damselfly flying in heathland bogs and streams.

The species is only 25–35mm long - a lot shorter than the Large Red Damselfly, with which it is sometimes confused. In both sexes the thorax is bronze-black on top.

The male has an entirely red abdomen; the female has a bronze-black abdomen with only the front and back of it red. A dark form has an almost entirely dark abdomen marked with pale segment divisors, the last two of which are reddish.

Thursley Common, in Surrey, was the first place I found them, but the best place in Southern England is the New Forest.

Downy Emerald

The Downy Emerald is metallic green and bronze in color, and its thorax is coated with fine hairs, hence its name. Like most other Emeralds, the Downy Emerald has bright shiny green eyes. Adults are around 5cm in length, and are in flight from May to July each year.

This species lives in woodlands near lakes and ponds; like other dragonflies, it lays eggs in water and its larvae are aquatic. It is distributed throughout most of Europe. Although it has been eliminated from some of its historic native areas in Britain due to habitat loss, dense populations of the Downy Emerald can still be found in its ideal locations.

It was a thrill to find my first Downy Emeralds - in a pond at Thursley Common in Surrey.

Portia Widow

The Portia Widow is a species of dragonfly in the family Libellulidae. It is found in many western, central and eastern African countries.

The species' natural habitats are dry savanna, moist savanna, subtropical or tropical dry shrubland, subtropical or tropical moist shrubland, rivers, shrub-dominated wetlands, swamps, freshwater lakes and marshes, and freshwater springs.

I found this unusual, but beautiful dragonfly in Gambia, West Africa.

Common Spreadwing

Inhabits ponds and marshes in the US and most of Canada, apart from Arctic regions.

Males tend to spend long periods quietly perched obliquely on emergent vegetation, flying only briefly. Females appear at wetlands when ready to breed.

My first introduction to a Common Spreadwing was beside Columbia Lake, in the grounds of Waterloo University in southern Ontario.

Four-spot Chaser

The Four-spot Chaser is a dragonfly of the family Libellulidae, found widely throughout Europe, Asia, and North America. I first found this Chaser on the Somerset Levels where it is very common.

This active dragonfly lives mainly by ponds, vernal pools, and slow flowing rivers, being most common in June and July.

The male is considered to be highly aggressive and will defend a given territory from incursions from other males of the species. The male likes prominent perches and will often return to the same perch on the margins of pools and ponds whilst it patrols for intruders.

Slaty Skimmer

The Slaty Skimmer is a dragonfly native to eastern United States and southern Ontario, Quebec, and New Brunswick. Mature males are dark blue with black heads. Females have brown abdomens with a darker stripe down their backs. Adults fly from June to August.

This species can be found at almost any quiet water with a muddy bottom, in or near a forest habitat and sometimes rivers. It feeds from twigs along forest edges, and the aggressive male can be active from 7am to 6.30pm, being most active in the morning.

It was great fun watching these highly active dragonflies around the shores of Orcan Lake in Eastern Ontario back in 2014.

American Rubyspot

I photographed this beautiful Damselfly on the shore of Columbia Lake near Waterloo, Ontario.

A large damselfly that inhabits the sunny sections of streams in the US and southern Canada, it perches on stream-side vegetation or exposed rocks. Males have a lustrous red head and thorax. The abdomen of both genders is brilliant green.

The name highlights this damselfly's status as the most widespread of the North American Rubyspots. It is reported from all of the lower 48 US states, except Washington and Idaho, and is also found in Mexico and southern and eastern Canada.

Small Red-eyed Damselfly

The Small Red-eyed Damselfly is a member of the family Coenagrionidae. It is very similar to the Red-eyed Damselfly.

This damselfly breeds in ponds, lakes and ditches and, in continental Europe, sluggish rivers. It seems to be well able to tolerate brackish water. It seems to be associated with floating vegetation such as Hornwort and Water Milfoil.

This was a surprise find on the Somerset Levels. I had previously thought it was the more common Red-eyed Damselfly until I looked more closely at my photographs.

Eastern Pondhawk

The Eastern Pondhawk, also known as the Common Pondhawk, is a dragonfly of the family Libellulidae, native to the eastern two-thirds of the United States, southern Ontario and Quebec, Canada. It is a dragonfly of ponds and still waters.

The species is distinguishable in that the female is bright green with a banded abdomen and the mature male has a blue abdomen with a green face and green and blue thorax.

I found this species beside Orcan Lake in eastern Ontario. Its green colouration was beautiful and unusual in a dragonfly.

Keeled Skimmer

The Keeled Skimmer is common in central and southern Europe, marginally entering into Russia and North Africa. It is locally common in western Britain and Ireland.

The typical habitats of Orthetrum coerulescens are pools and streams in acidic heathland, where it is often seen alongside Golden-ringed Dragonflies. My first experience of them was at Thursley Common in Surrey.

Yellow-tailed Ashy Skimmer

It was a great pleasure to see these attractive dragonflies around my lodgings in Tamil Nadu, India, and I managed to get quite a few photographs in the process.

Yellow-tailed Ashy Skimmer is a species of dragonfly in the family Libellulidae. The species is common through much of its range which stretches through parts of South Asia, South-East Asia, and Oceania, including countries such as India, Indonesia, China, Australia, and Vietnam.

Yellow-tailed Ashy Skimmer, or 'Swamp-watcher' is found in terrestrial areas with standing water. This can include small ponds, rice fields or marshes where it breeds.

Common Green Darner

The Common Green Darner is a species of dragonfly in the family Aeshnidae. One of the most common and abundant species throughout North America, it is well known for its migration from the northern United States south into Texas and Mexico.

Females oviposit in aquatic vegetation, beneath the water surface. Adult darners catch insects on the wing including moths, mosquitoes and flies.

I first found this species beside Laurel Creek Lake in Southern Ontario.

Dot-tailed Whiteface

This is another North American species that I found at Laurel Creek.

The Dot-tailed Whiteface is a species of dragonfly in the family Libellulidae. It is also one of the most common and widespread in the genus Leucorrhinia.

The Dot-tailed Whiteface can be found near boggy and marshy ponds and lakes and beaver ponds. It also can be found by farm ponds that are known to be frequently disturbed, and enjoys basking in clearings on the ground or on twigs.

Club-tailed Dragonfly

This is a distinctive, medium-sized dragonfly in the family Gomphidae. It has black and yellow or green patterning. It is a scarce species in the UK, but it can be found in early summer beside silty sections of two or three rivers.

My first experience of Club-tailed Dragonfly was beside the Thames near Pangbourne, west of Reading, Berkshire.

The Gomphidae are a family of dragonflies commonly referred to as clubtails or club-tailed dragonflies. The family contains about 90 genera and 900 species found across North and South America, Europe, Asia, and Australia. The name refers to the club-like widening of the end of the abdomen. However, this club is usually less pronounced in females and is entirely absent in some species.

Strong Skimmer

Fairly large and robust, with a dark brown thorax, the Strong Skimmer has a light blue abdomen and a deep yellowish brown pterostigma patches on the wings.

The Strong, or Tough, Skimmer, is a species of dragonfly in the family Libellulidae. It likes bushy areas and It is found over large areas of Africa. Within its wide range of habitats are moist lowland forests, dry savanna, moist savanna, dry or moist shrubland, shrubby wetlands, swamps, freshwater lakes and freshwater marshes.

I was first came across the Strong Skimmer in Gambia, West Africa.

Northern Bluet

This damselfly species inhabits small well-vegetated ponds, bog ponds, pools, swamps and occasional sluggish streams in western North American, north central US states and eastern Canadian provinces. Enallagma annexum, the Northern Bluet, is a species of damselfly in the family Coenagrionidae.

I found this species in several places in Southern Ontario, Canada, including Laurel Creek Conservation, Luther Lake and the area around Columbia Lake on the campus of Waterloo University.

Ebony Jewelwing

Breed in the streams of northern North America. It perches on streamside vegetation, making forays over the water. Most common on shallow shaded streams with emergent vegetation, the Ebony Jewelwing is a species of broad-winged damselfly. One of about 150 species of Calopterygidae, it is found in the eastern US and southeastern Canada, ranging west to the Great Plains. Other common names include Black-winged Damselfly.

It is quite a common species in the area around Laurel Creek, Near Waterloo, Ontario. I found it there many times.

Orange-winged Dropwing

The male Orange-winged Dropwing is a medium-sized scarlet dragonfly with a broad reddish amber patch on the base of transparent wings. Its natural habitats are subtropical or tropical streams and rivers. It breeds in marshes, ponds, and lakes, and prefers to perch on exposed rocks, dry areas, and boulders in riverbeds.

I found this species near the costal town of Sotogrande in SE Spain.

Lancet Clubtail

The Lancet Clubtail is a species of dragonfly in the family Gomphidae. It is widespread and common throughout southern Manitoba, Ontario, and the northeastern United States.

The male's claspers are 'lancet' shaped, hence the common name. The body is black with green stripes on the thorax and green triangles on the abdomen. The last two abdominal segments have yellow patches on the outer edges. Their flight period is from June to July.

I photographed this species beside Orcan Lake in Eastern Ontario.

Broad Scarlet

This scarlet dragonfly is a common species in southern Europe and throughout Africa. It also occurs across western Asia as far as southern China. It is a very rare vagrant in Britain. Its first record in the country was in Cornwall in August 1995.

It inhabits a wide range of both running and standing waters, except those that are shaded. Adults may be found some distance from water in habitats ranging from desert to open woodland. It is absent from dense forest.

The author found this beautiful species in Gambia, West Africa, and in Andalucia, Spain.

Racket-tailed Emerald

A beautiful dragonfly, Dorocordulia libera, the Racket-tailed Emerald, is a species of dragonfly in the family Corduliidae found in North America.

It is often found away from the water, foraging around roads, paths and forest openings. They perch more often than other emeralds - on leaves, logs, rocks or the ground. Look for it around lakes, ponds, and slow-moving streams - usually with marshy or boggy shorelines. Racket-tails will often fly around humans, eating the insects that are attracted by them.

I've found this species in Ontario: at Luther Lake and, later, at Orcan Lake.

Azure Damselfly

The azure damselfly (Coenagrion puella) is a species of damselfly found in most of Europe. It is notable for its distinctive black and blue colouring. They are commonly found around ponds and lakesides during the summer.

This lovely Damsel is very common on the Somerset Levels, where I live. There are quite a few on my garden pond every year.

The species breeds in a wide range of standing waters, including those that are acidic or eutrophic, but preferring smaller, more sheltered sites. It is regularly found in garden ponds and small ditches on which another species, the Common Blue Damselfy, is usually absent.

Broad-bodied Chaser

The Broad-bodied Chaser is one of the most common dragonflies in Europe and central Asia. It is very distinctive with a broad, flattened abdomen and four wing patches.

Broad-bodied Chasers are seen near still-water lakes and ponds, feeding on many types of small insects. They occur in both bare and sunny locations, where it is often the first dragonfly to colonise new habitats such as newly created ponds and well vegetated ponds.

The flight period is from April to September but are mostly seen in May and June. Their flight is very fast as they dart and dive above the water. They are very territorial and will fight with rival males and any other dragonflies they happen to encounter.

I saw my first Broad-bodied Chasers in the New Forest, Hampshire, where they are quite common over the heathlands.

Southern Hawker

The Southern Hawker was one of the earliest dragonflies I remember. It used to fly freely over the meadows on a friend's farm. In my experience they are very inquisitive creatures and will come up to hover close to your face.

Central Europe is the species stronghold, although it is uncommon in Scotland and doesn't breed at all in Ireland. They are very common in southern and central England and Wales.

Southern Hawkers prefers non-acidic waters, breeding in water line vegetation in well-vegetated, small ponds - often in garden ponds. Hunts well away from water and may be found hawking along woodland rides well into the evening.

Blue-tailed Damselfly

The Blue-tailed Damselfly belongs to the family Coenagrionidae. It is a frequent breeder on my garden pond and can be found over most of Britain.

This species is present throughout Europe, where it is an extremely common species. It can be found in a wide range of lowland environments with standing and slow flowing waters, both brackish and polluted.

Violet Dropwing

My first encounter with a Violet Dropwing was in the south of Spain, in the province of Huelva, during a recent holiday. Its colour came as a delightful surprise and I managed a few photographs before it flew off.

The Violet Dropwing is a species of dragonfly in the family Libellulidae. It is found in most of Africa, the Middle East, Arabian Peninsula and southern Europe. These dragonflies are called dropwings because of their habit of immediately lowering their wings after landing on a perch.

Widow Skimmer

I have found this dragonfly quite commonly in Southern Ontario. A fully mature male is a fine site with its broad patterned wings.

Widow Skimmers live near warm waters. The water source could be a pond, marsh, small lake, or lagoon.

Unlike some other species, Widow Skimmer males leave the female by herself, 'widowing' her as she lays her eggs just under the surface of the water.

This species can be found commonly across the United States (except in the higher Rocky Mountains areas) and in southern Ontario and Quebec.

Black-shouldered Spinyleg

The Black-shouldered Spinyleg is a species of dragonflies in the family Gomphidae.

Like other spinylegs, the species has long spines on their legs that help in the capture of prey. True to their name, their shoulders are black. Their flight time is between late May and early September, from southern Manitoba to the US east coast as far south as Florida.

This species is usually found at medium to large rapid streams, rivers, windswept lakes and ponds with rocky shores.

I found Black-shouldered Spinyleg beside Orcan Lake in eastern Ontario, Canada.

Banded Demoiselle

The Banded Demoiselle is a large damselfly that lives along the edges of slow-flowing rivers and canals, still ponds and lakes, and among lush, damp vegetation. Its common name is derived from the distinctive 'fingerprint' mark on the male's wings.

It is quite a common, early-emerging, damselfly. I find it regularly, flying over local rivers and canals. Its fluttering flight makes it easy to spot.

The only other damselfly with coloured wings is the similar-looking Beautiful Demoiselle; however, this species lives on smaller, fast-flowing rivers, mainly in the west of the country. Males are very territorial, performing fluttering display flights to win over females.

Common Citril

The Common Citril is a species of damselfly in the family Coenagrionidae. Its common names include Common Orange, Common Pond Damsel and Orange Waxtail. It is widespread in Africa, with natural habitats such as rivers, shrubby wetlands, swamps; freshwater lakes, marshes and freshwater springs

The males are orange and green coloured whilst the females range from light brown to dark brown depending on their maturity. The darkened colours in females aid in reproduction.

My first encounter with Common Citrils was at a sewage plant in Gambia, West Africa.

Black-tailed Skimmer

The Black-tailed Skimmer is a dragonfly belonging to the family Libellulidae. It is very common in my neck of the woods, particularly over the nearby Somerset Levels.

This species is widespread in Europe and Asia but is absent in the north of Britain and the northern half of Fennoscandia.

Black-tailed Skimmers are found at any open water with bare patches along the shore where the patrolling males frequently rest in the sun. It favours lakes, slow rivers, ponds and sometimes marshy areas without dense riparian vegetation.

Red-veined Darter

This is a widespread and common species in much of central and southern Europe including most Mediterranean islands. It is resident in the south of its European range but in some years it migrates northward. From the 1990s onwards has increasingly been found in northwest Europe, including Belgium, Sweden, Finland, Poland, Britain and Ireland.

Red-veined Darters breed in a wide range of habitats including marshes, lakes, ponds, permanent and seasonal rivers. It is able to recolonize dry areas after a rainfall. I first found this species in forest pools and streams in Gambia, West Africa.

Brilliant Emerald

The Brilliant Emerald is a middle-sized species of dragonfly. It is the largest and greenest of the Somatochlora species.

This beautiful dragonfly is found across most of northern Eurasia where it is the commonest of its genus. In Great Britain, it is locally common in south east England and has a very restricted population in Scotland. It breeds in neutral or acidic ponds and lakes flanked partially with trees. Woodland is usually close by.

I searched for Brilliant Emeralds on heathland in northwest Hampshire and was delighted to find them on a secluded woodland lake.

Western Clubtail

The Western Clubtail is a species in the family Gomphidae. It is found in Western Europe, although absent in the United Kingdom. Its natural habitats are clean ponds and canals, clay and mud holes.

The species is the only Gomphidae that lacks the 'club-shaped' abdomen, in spite of its name. It emerges early in spring, can be seen as soon as the end of March in the South of France, and flies until August depending on the location.

The species is reasonably common in Spain, where I found it during a visit in 2006.

Julia Skimmer

The Julia Skimmer is found throughout much of Africa including Gambia in West Africa, where I found it in 2011.

These insects are typically narrow-bodied, the wings delicately veined and transparent, held horizontally and flat when at rest. Descriptions may vary depending on where the insect is sighted because the species has several subspecies across Africa.

This dragonfly is a common sight along rivers and streams near woodland habitats. They face several threats, including water pollution and habitat destruction.

Common Blue Damselfly

The Common Blue Damselfly is common in many countries including Russia, Europe and South Korea. They are very frequent in my area of Somerset.

These damselflies inhabit freshwater bodies where conditions are favourable; they have also been seen in acidic fens as well as eutrophic ponds.

Variable Damselfly

The Variable Damselfly likes well-vegetated grazing marsh ditches, ponds, lakes and canals. It tends to favour sites with much more emergent vegetation that the Azure Damselfly, which is very similar.

It has a strangely disjointed distribution in the UK, but is more common in Ireland. I manage to find Variables all across the nearby Somerset Levels.

Twelve-spot Skimmer

The Twelve-Spotted Skimmer is a common North American dragonfly, also found in southern Canada and in all 48 of the US states.

It is a large species with three brown spots on each wing. In adult males, additional white spots form between the brown ones and at the bases of the hindwings.

Ponds, Lakes, and slow streams are the Twelve-spotted Skimmer's favourite breeding haunt as well as, occasionally, marshes or bogs.

I found this species on Columbia Lake in the grounds of Waterloo University in Canada.

Ditch Jewel

The Ditch Jewel is a species of dragonfly in the family Libellulidae. It is found in many Asian countries. I found it beside a lake in Tamil Nadu, India.

It breeds in weedy ponds, lakes, and slowly moving streams; especially in sluggish waters. It is very common along sewage canals, tanks, ponds and ditches.

Scarce Chaser

The Scarce Chaser is a species of dragonfly which is considered a species of special concern in Great Britain due to loss of its specific ideal habitat.

This species lives on floodplains and marshes with dense, abundant vegetation, and females deposit their eggs in slow-current streams. Once deposited by the female, the eggs lie embedded in the mud of the riverbed and the larvae develop underwater for usually two years. Adults live from May to August.

The species can be found in several locations in Somerset, my home county.

Southern Migrant Hawker

The Southern Migrant Hawker can be found hawking along damp reedy ditches in the UK. In its normal Mediterranean habitat it breeds in standing water.

This rare migrant appears to be becoming more frequent in the UK, and is a potential colonist. After a single confirmed record during the twentieth century, four individuals were observed in southern England during 2006. During 2010 many individuals were then seen in south Essex and north Kent, with oviposition being noted at two sites.

I came across this species at Priddy Mineries in North Somerset.

Slender Spreadwing

Often found well away from water in Eastern and central US and eastern Canada. Slender Spreadwings perch low in vegetation along woodland roads and trails. Avoids open water and prefers shady areas. It is native to eastern North America, including eastern Canada and the United States.

This damselfly is long and thin and lives around springs and drying ponds. It is common at Laurel Creek Conservation in southern Ontario, Canada, where I found it.

Blue-fronted Dancer

Found on broad muddy rivers, ponds and lakes in central and eastern US states, and southern Canada. The Blue-fronted Dancer is a species of damselfly in the family Coenagrionidae, native to parts of North America.

I found this beautiful species beside a stream on Waterloo University campus in southern Ontario.

Common Hawker

The Common Hawker, Moorland Hawker or Sedge Darner is one of the larger species of hawker dragonflies. It is native from Ireland to Japan and northern North America, with a flight period from June to early October.

This species breeds in acidic or neutral standing waters ranging from lakes to boggy pools on moorland and heathland up to a 600m altitude. It is common and widespread in northern and western Britain and Ireland.

I have met with Common Hawkers at Priddy Mineries on regular occasions.

Common Darter

The Common Darter is a dragonfly of the family Libellulidae, native to Eurasia. It is one of the most common dragonflies in Europe, occurring in a wide variety of water bodies, though with a preference for breeding in still water such as ponds and lakes. In the south of its range adults are on the wing all year round.

The species is very common in the UK. They are regular in my garden and throughout the rest of Somerset.

Variable Dancer

The Variable Dancer is a damselfly of the family Coenagrionidae. It is native to North America where it is widespread throughout the east, and also present in the interior western United States.

The male of the subspecies A.f.violacea (the Violet Dancer) is purple with a blue tip.

It inhabits central and eastern US and eastern provinces of Canada. Variable Dancers are most common on vegetated streams and small ponds.

I discovered Variable Dancers in lakeside grasses at Snyder Flats, southern Ontario.

Goblet-marked Damselfly

The Goblet-marked Damselfly is a medium-sized blue-and-black (or green-and-black) damselfly in the family Coenagrionidae. It's a fairly common species in the South and West of Europe but is not found in the British Isles, Scandinavia or Eastern Europe.

It can also be found in Asia, the Russian Federation and also in Africa. I discovered the species beside a small lake in Huelva Province, Spain.

Calico Pennant

The Calico Pennant is a beautiful species of dragonfly in the family Libellulidae. It is native to eastern Canada and eastern United States.

This species lives near calm water bodies surrounded by vegetation. My photograph was taken in the Laurel Creek Conservation, southern Ontario.

Swamp Darner

The Swamp Darner is a species in the dragonfly family Aeshnidae. It is a large dragonfly of southern swamps on the Caribbean and North America.

As well as swamps this species inhabits wooded ponds and shaded sluggish streams. I came across Swamp Darners in a forest near the shores of Lake Erie in Canada.

Chalk-fronted Corporal

The Chalk-fronted Corporal is a skimmer dragonfly found in the northern US and southern Canada.

Chalk-fronted Corporals often perch horizontally on the ground or on floating objects in the water, flying up to take prey from the air. They readily approach humans to feed on the mosquitoes and biting flies that thay attract.

I managed to photograph this species at Luther Lake in southern Ontario.

Small Pincertail

The Small Pincertail, or Green-eyed Hook-tailed Dragonfly, is a species of dragonfly belonging to the family Gomphidae. It is a quite common and widespread dragonfly, present in most of Europe and in North Africa (Algeria, Morocco, Tunisia).

These dragonflies usually inhabit clean rivers with some faster running water and gravel or sandy banks. Occasionally they also occur at large lakes. My introduction to them was in the Pyrenean foothills of northern Spain.

Southern Damselfly

The Southern Damselfly is a species of damselfly in the family Coenagrionidae. It is found over much of Europe and Mediterranean North Africa. Its natural habitats are rivers and freshwater springs, but it is threatened by habitat loss.

The species requires areas of open vegetation, mixed with slow flowing water in which to lay their eggs.

The New Forest in Hampshire is where I regularly find Southern Damselflies.

Common Whitetail

The Common Whitetail, with its striking and unusual appearance, is found across much of North America. The species can be seen hawking for mosquitoes and other small flying insects over ponds, marshes, and slow-moving rivers in most regions except the higher mountains.

Like all perchers, common whitetails often rest on objects near water, and sometimes on the ground. I have found them in among the grasses and waterside vegetation of Waterloo University in southern Ontario.

Large Red Damselfly

The Large Red Damselfly is a species of damselfly belonging to the family Coenagrionidae. It is mainly a European damselfly with some populations in northern Africa and west Asian countries.

These Damselflies inhabit small ponds, lakes and dikes, and occasionally slow-moving rivers. They tend to avoid fast flowing water. The species is quite common in my garden and in many regions of the UK and Europe.

Blue Percher

The Blue Percher is a species of dragonfly in the family Libellulidae, also known as the Chalky Percher or Ground Skimmer. It is found in China, Japan, India, New Guinea and Australia.

This is a small dragonfly with bluish eyes and greenish-yellow or olivaceous thorax, and black marks on its abdomen. It breeds in ponds, wet rice fields, shallow lakes, drainage ditches and similar habitats. It is one of the most common dragonflies in Asia, found in both the plains and hills, and in dry and wet areas.

I found this species among the grasses at Auroville in Tamil Nadu, India.

Migrant Hawker

The Migrant Hawker is one of the smaller species of hawker dragonflies. It can be found away from water, but for breeding it prefers still or slow-flowing water and can tolerate brackish sites. The flight period is from July to the end of October. The species occurs in North Africa, southern and central Europe to the Baltic region. It is a common dragonfly in my area of Somerset.

The Migrant Hawker is a small aeshna species which appears dark in flight. It is similar in appearance to other aeshnas but has a characteristic 'golf-tee' shaped mark on the second segment of the abdomen, which is diagnostic. In flight it looks like a small Emperor Dragonfly with a blue abdomen which, when seen from the side, curves downwards.

Sedge Sprite

The Sedge Sprite is a delicate metallic green damselfly of damp grassland. It frequents marshes, marshy ponds, fens and vernal pools.

The species perches horizontally or obliquely on vegetation. It rarely flies over open water, preferring to skulk low in dense vegetation where its small size and green colouration make it difficult to see.

I found Sedge Sprites in various locations around Waterloo, in southern Ontario.

White-faced Meadowhawk

The White-faced Meadowhawk is a dragonfly in the genus Sympetrum. It is found in the northern United States and southern Ontario. Adult males are identifiable by a distinctive pure white face and red bodies.

I have discovered this attractive species in wooded areas around the Grand River and Waterloo areas of southern Ontario.

Beautiful Demoiselle

The Beautiful Demoiselle is a European damselfly belonging to the family Calopterygidae. It is most at home along fast-flowing waters. I have found them in New Forest woodland edges and in scrubby areas of the Somerset Levels.

The species' range covers all of Europe with the exception of the south western Iberian Peninsula, the Balearic Islands and Iceland. In the north it extends to the Arctic polar sea.

The Beautiful Demoiselle is mostly found in lowland locations, but regular findings come from areas up to a maximum height of 980m above sea level. Occasionally they may be found at heights of up to 1200m, such as in the Alps.

Hairy Hawker

The Hairy Hawker lives in ponds, lakes, fens, ditches, and canals rich in vegetation. It requires open and sunny areas with dense vegetation for protection. Here they are able to feed on flying insects, shelter, and sexually mature.

The species is susceptible to poor ditch management and water conditions. This is the reason the species disappeared for a few years, only to return recently. The Hairy Dragonfly will only fly in sunshine and will hastily retreat if the sun happens to go in.

Hairy Hawkers are relatively common where I live, on the Somerset wetlands.

Swamp Spreadwing

The Swamp Spreadwing is a damselfly of the genus Lestes. It ranges from eastern North America west to Minnesota, Oklahoma, and Texas, and to Georgia and South Carolina. It is most commonly seen between May and October.

Its habitat is primarily small, well-vegetated ponds, but also marshes, swamps, and sluggish backwaters. It perches low on emergent or shoreline vegetation, flying only short distances.

My photograph shows one of this species beside Columbia Lake, Waterloo, Canada.

Copper Demoiselle

This is a species of damselfly in the family Calopterygidae, known by the common names Copper Demoiselle or Mediterranean Demoiselle.

It lives along rivers and streams, but also in sunny larger waters, though it may be affected by habitat changes such as water pollution.

I found Copper Demoiselles beside the Rio Guardiaro near Gaucin, Spain.

Black Darter

Sympetrum danae, the Black Darter, is a dragonfly found in northern Europe, Asia, and North America. Apart from Damselflies, it is Britain's smallest resident dragonfly, and a very active late summer insect typical of heathland and moorland bog pools.

Members of the genus Sympetrum are known as darters in the UK and as meadowhawks in the US and Canada. I have found the Black Darter regularly around heathland pools and boggy ground.

White Corporal

The White Corporal is a species in the family Libellulidae. It has a fairly small range, only found in the north eastern US and south eastern Canada. Their flight period is in May-June.

The species' habitats include muddy-bottomed ponds, lakes and bogs. It also likes gently flowing water such as lake inlets, particularly with emergent plants or lilies. It perches on the ground, tree trunks or floating objects.

My photograph was taken at Luther Lake in southern Ontario, Canada.

Orange Featherleg

The Orange Featherleg is a species of damselfly in the family Platycnemididae. It is the only adult European damselfly which combines an orange-red abdomen and blue eyes.

The species lives in fresh water, either still or up to moderately fast-flowing. It is common across southwest Europe including Portugal, Spain, and France, but there are, however, some recent records from Germany.

I found this species on the banks of the Rio Guardiaro in Andalucia, Spain.

Red-waisted Whiteface

The Red-waisted Whiteface is a species of dragonfly in the family Libellulidae. It is found across Canada as far north as Alaska and south to northern parts of the United States. This species is similar to the frosted whiteface, with the same white pruinose color on the base of the abdomen, except that it is slightly larger and more slender.

My first encounter with this species was at Luther Lake Conservation in southern Ontario.

Spectacled Skimmer

The Spectacled Skimmer is a species of dragonfly in the family Libellulidae. It is found in most of sub Sahara Africa. Its natural habitats are a mix of subtropical or tropical moist lowland forests, dry shrubland, subtropical or moist shrubland, and rivers.

My photo was taken in Gambia, West Africa.

Printed in Poland
by Amazon Fulfillment
Poland Sp. z o.o., Wrocław